# the fondue party cookbook

D1040516

# the fondue party cookbook

## beth merriman

**Published in Association with**
*Parade Magazine*

GROSSET & DUNLAP
A National General Company

*Publishers*       *New York*

Copyright © 1971 by Beth Merriman
LIBRARY OF CONGRESS CATALOG NUMBER: 70-144058
ISBN: 0-448-02079-3 (paper ed.)
ISBN: 0-448-02464-0 (hard cover ed.)
ALL RIGHTS RESERVED
PUBLISHED SIMULTANEOUSLY IN CANADA

PRINTED IN THE UNITED STATES OF AMERICA

# Table of Contents

# Introduction

The vogue for fondue parties has spread like wild-fire from coast to coast. Hostesses have discovered that they can entertain with a minimum of effort and a maximum of fun. A variety of fondue sets are on sale everywhere, from mail-order houses to exclusive specialty shops—just select one in line with your budget.

Sometimes it is a problem to know what to serve before and after the fondue and that is why this book was written. You will find menu suggestions for a variety of parties and recipes for foods other than fondues that are included in these menus (a recipe is provided for each starred item in the menu). In most cases, the preparation can be done well ahead of time, to give you a chance to have fun at your own party! To make up menus of your own, use the index as a helpful guide to recipes for salads, desserts and other delights.

*Beth Merriman*

# the fondue party cookbook

# 1.
# Cheese Fondues

THIS delightful dish originated in Switzerland, so naturally the main ingredient in the classic recipe is well-aged Emmenthaler or Gruyère Swiss cheese, or both. Emmenthaler alone makes a fondue of the mildest flavor. Half and half gives a stronger flavor, while Gruyère alone is strongest.

Cut the cheese into small pieces or shred it and it will melt more smoothly than when it is grated.

The wine you use should be selected with care. It should be dry and light with a lively flavor, e.g., Rhine, Riesling, Neuchâtel or Chablis. If the wine is not tart enough add about 1½ teaspoons of lemon juice for every half pound of cheese.

A liqueur is often added, usually kirsch, which is a cherry brandy. However, you may prefer cognac, light rum or applejack.

Select crusty French bread for dunking and cut it so that each piece has crust on two sides, so that the fondue fork can catch and hold it.

The proper equipment is essential for a successful fondue. At first the cooking is done over direct low heat. The wine is heated until tiny air bubbles form (this is *not* boiling—never let wine boil). Next, the cheese is added, about ½ cup at a time, while stirring. Each batch of cheese must melt before the next is added and stirring must not cease. Last of all, the seasonings are added, and the liqueur, if used.

At this point the fondue is transferred to a heat-proof casserole. (This will not be necessary if you have a round casserole that can be set over direct heat on the stove and then transferred to the warmer, or if you own a fondue set that is heat-controlled and can be used for both processes. In either case, don't forget to rub the casserole with garlic before you start.) The casserole is then set over a warmer. A candle will not give off enough heat, so the fuel should be alcohol, canned heat (Sterno), butane gas or electricity. Be sure you know how to control the heat to keep the fondue bubbling gently.

If the fondue should get too thick, warm a little wine and add it. Sometimes, if the cheese has not aged long enough, or if cooking and stirring are carelessly done, the fondue may separate or get lumpy. If this happens, blend ½ teaspoon of corn-starch with a little warm wine, add it to the fondue and stir with a wire whisk until smooth.

Now for the fun. Place the fondue pot in the middle of the table. Provide each guest, not more than four or five to a table, with a long-handled fondue fork. Tell them how to spear the bread and dunk it with a figure eight stir (one at a time). This method keeps the fondue stirred as it bubbles. If you are having more than five guests, have two fondue pots ready and prepare the recipe twice.

When the fondue is almost gone a rich brown crust will form on the bottom of the casserole. This delicious delicacy may be divided and shared or it can be given as a prize to the one who hasn't dropped a single piece of bread into the fondue!

# CHRISTMAS EVE PARTY

Cheese Fondue*
Jellied Lima Bean Salad*
Frozen Pudding Ice Cream
Swedish Spritz Cookies*
Coffee

# Cheese Fondue

½ pound Emmen-
thaler, shredded
½ pound Gruyère,
shredded
1 garlic clove,
slashed
2 cups dry white
wine

3 tablespoons kirsch
1 teaspoon cornstarch
Nutmeg
White pepper
Chunks of French
bread

Combine cheeses. Rub heavy saucepan with garlic clove. Pour in wine. Heat until air bubbles form. Add cheese gradually, stirring constantly. Continue to stir until smooth. Blend kirsch and cornstarch; stir in. Continue to cook and stir until mixture begins to thicken. Season to taste with nutmeg and pepper. Transfer to heatproof earthenware casserole; set over warmer. Spear bread chunks on long forks; dip into fondue. *Makes 4 servings.*

# Jellied Lima Bean Salad

1 envelope un-flavored gelatin
½ cup cold water
1 cup boiling water
¼ cup sugar
1 teaspoon salt
½ teaspoon Ac'cent
2 tablespoons lemon juice
Few drops Tabasco
¼ cup vinegar
Green food coloring
1 tablespoon grated onion
1 tablespoon celery seed
2 cups cooked lima beans
Watercress
Mayonnaise
Pimiento strips

Sprinkle gelatin on cold water. Dissolve in boiling water. Add sugar, salt, Ac'cent, lemon juice, Tabasco and vinegar; stir until sugar dissolves. Tint to desired shade of green with food coloring. Chill until consistency of unbeaten egg white. Fold in onion, celery seed and lima beans. Spoon into individual molds. Chill until set. Unmold. Serve with watercress and mayonnaise. Garnish with strips of pimiento. *Makes 4 to 6 servings.*

# Swedish Spritz Cookies

1 ½ cups butter or margarine
1 cup sugar
1 egg, well beaten
2 teaspoons vanilla
4 cups sifted all-purpose flour
1 teaspoon baking powder

Cream butter or margarine; add sugar gradually, while continuing to cream. Add egg and vanilla. Beat well. Mix and sift flour and baking powder; add. Mix to smooth dough. Chill thoroughly. Force through cookie press, forming Christmas designs, or roll and cut in any desired shape. Bake at 400° until set but not brown, about 8 to 10 minutes. *Makes about 4 dozen.*

# TREE-TRIMMING PARTY

Fontina*
Red Apple and Grapefruit Salad
Raisin Cream Dressing*
Coffee

## Fontina

| | |
|---|---|
| 1 tablespoon butter or margarine | 1 pound Swiss cheese, grated |
| 3 tablespoons flour | Salt, pepper, nutmeg |
| 2 cups milk | Chunks of French bread |

Melt butter; blend in flour. Add milk gradually. Bring almost to boiling point; add cheese gradually, stirring constantly, until all cheese is melted and mixture is smooth. Season to taste with salt, pepper and nutmeg. Transfer to heatproof earthenware casserole; set over warmer. Spear bread on long forks and dunk. *Makes 4 servings.*

## Raisin Cream Dressing

| | |
|---|---|
| ½ cup seedless raisins | 2 tablespoons vinegar |
| 1 cup dairy sour cream | ½ teaspoon dry mustard |
| 1 tablespoon sugar | ⅛ teaspoon salt |

Rinse raisins in boiling water. Drain; chop. Whip cream thick, not stiff. Combine sugar, vinegar, mustard and salt; whip slowly into cream. Fold in raisins. *Makes 6 servings.*

5

# TWELFTH NIGHT PARTY

Raw Vegetable Relishes
Assorted Crackers
Cheese Fondue (p. 3)
Kirsch or White Wine
Eggnog Tapioca*
Mt. Vernon Fruit Cake*

## Eggnog Tapioca

2 eggs, separated
4 tablespoons sugar, divided
2 cups milk, divided
3 tablespoons quick-cooking tapioca
⅛ teaspoon salt
1 teaspoon rum flavoring
Nutmeg

Beat egg yolks; add 2 tablespoons sugar and ½ cup milk. Add tapioca and remaining milk. Cook over low or medium heat, stirring constantly, until mixture boils, about 5 minutes. (The mixture will be thin.) Remove from heat; cool. Add salt and flavoring. Beat egg whites until foamy, gradually add remaining sugar, beating constantly until stiff peaks form; fold into tapioca mixture. Pour into serving dish; chill. Sprinkle with nutmeg. *Makes 6 servings.*

## Mt. Vernon Fruit Cake

1 cup butter or margarine
1 cup extra fine (instant) sugar
5 eggs, separated
2½ cups sifted all-purpose flour
1 teaspoon mace
¼ teaspoon nutmeg
1 cup diced candied fruits
½ cup golden seedless raisins
2 tablespoons red wine
2 teaspoons brandy flavoring

Cream butter or margarine until consistency of mayonnaise. Add sugar gradually, then egg yolks; cream until light and fluffy. Mix and sift flour and spices; combine with fruits; add. Add wine and brandy flavoring. Beat egg whites stiff; fold in. Spoon into greased and floured 9-inch tube cake pan. Bake at 325° for 1 hour and 15 minutes, or until done. Cool on rack. Frost and decorate if desired.

## AFTER-THE-GAME SUPPER

Hot Tomato Juice
Cheese Fondue (p. 3)
Roman Salad*
Rum Chocolate Cream Pie*
Coffee

## Roman Salad

1 large head iceberg lettuce, chopped
4 hard-cooked eggs, sliced
1 cup chopped dill pickles
4 medium-sized tomatoes, sliced and quartered

Rings from 1 large sweet onion
⅔ cup vegetable oil
⅓ cup vinegar
2 tablespoons lemon juice
2 garlic cloves, crushed
2 teaspoons seasoned salt
2 eggs, raw

Combine lettuce, hard-cooked eggs, pickles, tomatoes and onion rings. Combine oil, vinegar, lemon juice, garlic and seasoned salt; mix well. Pour oil mixture over lettuce mixture; toss lightly but thoroughly. Break raw eggs into lettuce mixture; toss until all traces of egg disappear. *Makes 8 to 12 servings*

# Rum Chocolate Cream Pie

4 cups milk, divided
2 tablespoons butter or margarine
1 cup sugar
2 squares unsweetened chocolate, melted
6 tablespoons cornstarch
4 egg yolks, slightly beaten
½ teaspoon salt
2 tablespoons rum
1 10-inch baked pie shell
1 cup whipping cream

Combine ¾ cup milk, butter and sugar. Stir over low heat until mixture comes to a boil. Add melted chocolate; mix well. Blend cornstarch to thin paste with a little of the cold milk; stir in remaining cold milk; add to chocolate mixture slowly while stirring. Cook and stir until well thickened. Cook for 10 minutes without stirring. Add hot mixture to egg yolks; mix well; return to saucepan; add salt; cook and stir for 1 minute. Remove from heat; add rum. Spoon into baked pie shell. Chill until firm. Whip cream; swirl on pie. Garnish with chocolate curls if desired.

## WATCH NIGHT PARTY

Fresh Fruit Salad
(Apples, Grapes, Grapefruit, Oranges, etc.)
Honey French Dressing*
Classic Cheese Fondue (p. 10)
Innkeeper's Pie*
Coffee

# Honey French Dressing

1 ½ tablespoons strained honey
3 tablespoons cider vinegar
4 tablespoons vegetable oil
¼ teaspoon salt
1 teaspoon paprika
Dash cayenne

Put honey, vinegar, oil, salt, paprika and cayenne in covered jar. Shake well before serving. *Makes 6 servings.*

# Innkeeper's Pie

1 ½ squares unsweetened chocolate
½ cup water
⅔ cup sugar
¼ cup butter or margarine
2 teaspoons vanilla, divided
1 cup sifted all-purpose flour
¾ cup sugar
1 teaspoon baking powder
½ teaspoon salt
¼ cup soft shortening
½ cup milk
1 egg
1 unbaked 9-inch pie shell with high rim
½ cup chopped walnuts

Melt chocolate in water; add ⅔ cup sugar. Bring to boil, stirring constantly. Remove from heat. Stir in butter and 1 ½ teaspoons vanilla. Set aside. Mix and sift flour, ¾ cup sugar, baking powder and salt. Add shortening, milk and ½ teaspoon vanilla. Beat 2 minutes. Add egg; beat 2 minutes. Pour batter into unbaked pie shell. Stir chocolate sauce and pour carefully over batter. Sprinkle top with nuts. Bake at 350° for 55 to 60 minutes or until cake tester inserted in center comes out clean.

# APRES SKI PARTY

Classic Cheese Fondue*
Mixed Green Salad
Cointreau Chiffon Pie*
Coffee

## Classic Cheese Fondue

¾ pound Emmen-
    thaler or Gruyère
    cheese, or a com-
    bination of both,
    shredded
2 tablespoons flour
1 ½ cups dry white wine
1 tablespoon lemon
    juice (optional)

1 garlic clove, peeled
    and slashed
Salt
Fresly ground
    black pepper
2 to 3 tablespoons
    kirsch
Chunks of French
    or Italian bread

Toss cheese and flour together until all trace of flour disappears. Pour wine and lemon juice into fondue pot. Add garlic clove; heat until air bubbles begin to form. Add cheese, handful by handful, stirring constantly with a fork until smooth. Add salt and freshly ground pepper to taste. Discard garlic. Stir in 2 tablespoons (or more) of kirsch. Spear bread cubes on fondue forks and dunk in the cheese sauce with a stirring motion.

## Cointreau Chiffon Pie

1 envelope un-
    flavored gelatin
¼ cup cold water
4 eggs, separated
¾ cup sugar, divided
⅓ cup orange juice

¼ teaspoon salt
2 tablespoons
    Cointreau
1 tablespoon grated
    orange peel
1 9-inch baked pie
    shell

10

Soften gelatin in cold water. Beat egg yolks until thick and lemon-colored; beat in ½ cup sugar, orange juice and salt. Cook over boiling water, stirring constantly until thickened. Add softened gelatin; stir until gelatin dissolves. Add Cointreau and orange peel. Cool until mixture begins to stiffen. Beat egg whites; add remaining sugar gradually; beat until stiff and glossy; fold into gelatin mixture. Spoon into baked pie shell. Chill until firm. Garnish top with whipped cream.

## CARD PARTY SUPPER

California Salad Bowl*
Fondue with Ripe Olives*
Strawberries and Cream
Angel Food Cake

## California Salad Bowl

| | |
|---|---|
| 2 heads iceberg lettuce | ¼ cup crumbled blue cheese |
| ¼ cup garlic-flavored vegetable oil (see below) | ½ teaspoon dry mustard |
| ½ cup vegetable oil | ⅓ cup lemon juice |
| 1 tablespoon Worcestershire sauce | 1 egg |
| Salt and pepper | 2 cups toast croutons (see below) |
| ½ cup grated hard cheese, such as Romanelle | |

Break lettuce in large salad bowl. Add oils, Worcestershire, a sprinkle of salt and pepper, cheeses, mustard and lemon juice. Break raw egg into bowl. Toss until lettuce is thoroughly coated. Dip croutons in additional garlic-flavored oil; drain and add to salad just before serving. *Makes 8 large servings.*

***Garlic-flavored vegetable oil:***
Cut 4 garlic cloves into 1 cup vegetable oil; let stand for several hours until oil is well flavored. Remove garlic. (Save any unused oil for next salad.)

***Toast Croutons:***
Cut trimmed bread slices into ½-inch cubes; measure 2 cups. Toast in 350° oven until golden brown and crisp, stirring often for even browning.

## Fondue with Ripe Olives

1 package (12 ounces) process Swiss cheese
1 cup dry white wine
⅛ teaspoon nutmeg
1 garlic clove
1 ½ cups canned pitted ripe olives
Chunks of French bread

Grate cheese or break into small pieces. Heat wine and nutmeg until air bubbles begin to form. Add cheese, small amounts at a time, stirring until mixture is smooth. Rub earthenware casserole with garlic clove; transfer cheese mixture to casserole. Set over warmer. Thread ripe olives and bread chunks on skewers. Dip into fondue. *Makes about 1½ cups cheese dipping mixture.*

## PRE-FOOTBALL BRUNCH

Tossed Green Salad
Green Goddess Dressing*
Classic Cheese Fondue (p. 10)
Kirsch or White Wine
Baked Apples Grenada*
Coffee

# Green Goddess Dressing

¼ bunch water cress
¼ green pepper
12 sprigs parsley
¼ bunch scallions
  (spring onions)

1 garlic clove
1 can (2 ounces)
  anchovy fillets
1 quart mayonnaise

Put water cress, pepper, parsley, scallions, garlic and anchovies through food chopper, using fine knife. Combine with mayonnaise. Serve over mixed salad greens. Any left-over dressing may be refrigerated for later use.


# Baked Apples Grenada

4 large baking
  apples
Grenadine syrup
Hot water

½ cup whipping
  cream
2 tablespoons orange
  marmalade
Nutmeg

Core apples, being careful not to cut through blossom end. Pare about ⅓ of the way from stem to blossom end. Fill centers and brush cut surface with grenadine syrup. Place in baking dish; add hot water to the depth of about ½ inch; cover. Bake at 350° for about 45 minutes, or until apples are tender, brushing cut surface with grenadine once or twice more. Chill. When ready to serve, whip cream and fold in marmalade. Fill center of apples and sprinkle lightly with nutmeg.

13

# AFTER-THE-MOVIES

Caesar Salade Nouveau*
Swiss Fondue for Four*
Fudge Cake*
Coffee

## Caesar Salade Nouveau

3 quarts broken or
cut salad greens
(iceberg, romaine,
chicory, escarole,
etc.)
2 tablespoons butter
or margarine
1 crushed garlic
clove
¾ cup wheat germ
Whole leaves
romaine lettuce

2 eggs
¼ cup lemon juice
½ cup vegetable oil
¼ cup wine vinegar
1 tablespoon Wor-
cestershire sauce
¼ cup shredded
Parmesan cheese
1 can (2 ounces)
anchovy fillets
(not rolled)
Coarse black pepper

Cut iceberg lettuce into bite-size chunks; break or tear leaf lettuce, romaine, chicory, escarole, etc. (any desired combination) into small pieces.
Melt butter in small saucepan; add crushed garlic. Cook over low heat 5 minutes; stir in wheat germ; set aside. Line salad bowl with whole leaves of romaine. Fill bowl with broken or cut greens. Break 2 eggs on greens. Combine next 4 ingredients; beat with rotary beater; pour over greens. Toss until all traces of egg disappear. Add cheese, anchovies, garlic wheat germ mixture and a sprinkling of coarse black pepper. Toss again until well-mixed. Serve while the fondue cooks. *Makes 8 to 10 servings.*
14

# Swiss Fondue for Four

½ pound Emmen-
thaler cheese,
shredded
1 ½ tablespoons flour
1 garlic clove,
slashed
1 cup dry white
wine

½ teaspoon salt
⅛ teaspoon pepper
Dash nutmeg
3 tablespoons kirsch
Chunks of French
bread

Dredge cheese with flour. Rub earthenware casserole with clove of garlic. Pour wine into pan; set
over low heat. When air bubbles rise to surface (before boiling point) stir with fork. Add cheese by hand-
fuls; stir until each handful melts before adding the
next. Stir until mixture starts bubbling lightly; add
salt, pepper and nutmeg. Stir in kirsch; mix thoroughly. To serve: Transfer to earthenware casserole;
set over warmer; keep bubbling lightly while dunking
bread. Keep heat low. *Makes 4 servings.*

# Fudge Cake

2 squares un-
sweetened
chocolate
1 cup boiling water,
divided
1 cup sugar
2 tablespoons veg-
etable oil
1 egg

1 ½ cups sifted all-
purpose flour
1 teaspoon baking
powder
1 teaspoon baking
soda
½ teaspoon salt
1 teaspoon vanilla

Melt chocolate over hot water. Add ½ cup boiling water; stir until custard-like in consistency. Remove from heat. Add sugar and oil; mix well. Beat
egg; add. Mix and sift dry ingredients; stir in. Add
vanilla. Add remaining boiling water. Spoon into

15

greased 8-inch square cake pan. Bake at 350° for 45 to 50 minutes. Cool on cake rack. Split into 2 layers. Fill and frost as desired.

## LUNCHEON FOR FOUR

Chilled Tomato Juice
Golden Buck*
Green Peas with Onions
Quick Lemon Pie*
Coffee          Tea

## Golden Buck

Serve Fontina (p. 5) on toast slices topped with a poached egg. Garnish with mushrooms.

## Quick Lemon Pie

| | |
|---|---|
| 1 can (15 ounces) sweetened condensed milk | 2 egg yolks |
| | 1 8-inch baked pie shell |
| ½ cup lemon juice | 2 egg whites |
| Grated peel 1 lemon | 6 tablespoons sugar |

Combine condensed milk, lemon juice, lemon peel and egg yolks. Pour into baked pie shell. Beat egg whites stiff; add sugar gradually while continuing to beat. Swirl on pie. Bake at 325° for 20 minutes.

## BON VOYAGE PARTY

Caerphilly Fondue*
Bavarian Fruit Slaw*
Chocolate Pudding
Suspiros*
Coffee

# Caerphilly Fondue

2 tablespoons but-
ter or margarine
2 tablespoons flour
½ teaspoon salt
Freshly ground
black pepper

Dash Tabasco
sauce
1 ½ cups milk
2 cups shredded
Caerphilly cheese
Toast fingers

Melt butter in top of double boiler. Add flour, salt,
pepper and Tabasco. Stir until flour and butter are
smoothly blended. Add milk, stirring constantly
until sauce is smooth. Add cheese. Stir continuously,
in one direction only, until cheese is melted. Serve
immediately on toast fingers. *Makes 4 servings.*

# Bavarian Fruit Slaw

1 cup sliced apples
2 bananas
½ cup French
dressing

3 cups shredded
red cabbage
1 cup sliced celery

Slice apples and bananas; drop immediately into
French dressing to avoid discoloration. Combine
with remaining ingredients; toss with fork until
thoroughly mixed. *Makes 6 servings.*

# Suspiros

3 egg whites
1 cup sugar
½ teaspoon lemon
juice

½ cup slivered
blanched almonds

Beat egg whites until very stiff. Beat in sugar gradually. Add lemon juice. Fold in almonds. Line a
cookie sheet with foil. Drop mixture by teaspoons on
foil. Bake at 350° for 12 minutes. Remove when
slightly brown. *Makes about 12.*

# TEEN-AGERS GET TOGETHER

Swiss Fondue with Buttermilk*
Jellied Pineapple Salad*
Brownies a la Mode
Cola Beverage

## Swiss Fondue with Buttermilk

| | |
|---|---|
| 1 pound Emmenthaler cheese, shredded | ¼ teaspoon white pepper |
| 3 tablespoons cornstarch | ¼ teaspoon nutmeg |
| ½ teaspoon salt | 2 cups buttermilk |
| | 1 garlic clove |
| | 1 loaf French bread |

Toss cheese with cornstarch, salt, white pepper and nutmeg. Heat buttermilk with garlic clove over low heat. When hot, remove garlic. Add Swiss cheese, a handful at a time. Stir constantly after each addition until cheese is melted. Serve from an earthenware casserole set over a warmer. Each person serves himself from the common dish, dipping chunks of French bread, which are speared on long forks, into cheese sauce with a stirring motion.

## Jellied Pineapple Salad

| | |
|---|---|
| 1 envelope unflavored gelatin | 1 teaspoon salt |
| ½ cup cold water | ½ cup sugar |
| 1 can (1 pound) crushed pineapple | Green food coloring |
| ½ cup pineapple syrup from can | ½ cup diced cucumber |
| Juice of 1 lemon | Crisp salad greens |
| ⅓ cup vinegar | Mayonnaise |

Soften gelatin in cold water. Drain crushed pineapple; heat syrup. Add hot syrup to gelatin; stir
until dissolved. Strain lemon juice; add with vinegar,
salt and sugar. Stir until sugar dissolves. Add 1 or 2
drops green coloring; stir to obtain even color. Chill
until syrupy. Fold in crushed pineapple and cucumber. Pour into 1-quart mold. Chill until set. Unmold
on crisp salad greens. Garnish with mayonnaise.
*Makes 6 servings.*

# 2.
# Baked Cheese Fondues

BAKED fondues were born in this country and they have never ceased to be popular. And no wonder. They are delicious, nourishing, and, in most cases, economical.

A baked fondue would make a fine main dish for a progressive dinner party, for a welcome home supper, for a covered dish dinner or to take to a convalescent or to someone you know who has just moved into your neighborhood and hasn't unpacked the can opener!

20

# Baked Cheese Fondue I

2 ¼ cups milk
2 cups coarse day-old bread crumbs
2 ⅔ cups grated process American Cheddar cheese
1 teaspoon salt
Dash cayenne pepper
1 tablespoon bottled thick meat sauce
2 tablespoons minced onion
1 teaspoon dry mustard
4 eggs, separated

Scald milk; cool. Combine remaining ingredients, all but eggs, in large bowl. Add milk; mix well. Beat egg yolks until thick and lemon-colored. Slowly stir into bread mixture. Beat egg whites stiff, but not dry. Fold in. Pour into greased 2-quart casserole. Set in baking pan. Fill pan with warm water up to 1 inch from top of casserole. Bake at 325° for 1 ½ hours or until delicately browned and firm in center. *Makes 6 servings.*

# Baked Cheese Fondue II

2 cups milk
2 cups dry bread cubes
Dash cayenne
½ teaspoon dry mustard
1 teaspoon salt
⅛ teaspoon pepper
3 cups grated Cheddar cheese
4 eggs, separated

Scald milk; add bread cubes and seasonings. Add cheese; stir over low heat until melted. Stir a little of the cheese mixture into slightly beaten egg yolks. Stir into remaining cheese mixture; cool slightly. Beat egg whites until stiff but not dry. Fold into cheese mixture. Turn into 1 ½-quart greased casserole. Bake at 350° for 45 to 50 minutes. *Makes 6 servings.*

# Baked Cheese and Bacon Fondue

2 cups soft bread
    crumbs
1 cup shredded sharp
    Cheddar cheese
2 cups milk, scalded
Dash of pepper
1 teaspoon prepared
    mustard

1 teaspoon Wor-
    cestershire sauce
4 eggs, slightly
    beaten
¾ cup cooked,
    crumbled bacon

Place bread crumbs and cheese in shallow 1½-quart baking dish. Combine milk, pepper, mustard, Worcestershire and eggs; pour over bread crumbs and cheese; add bacon. Bake at 350° for 25 minutes or until set and lightly browned. *Makes 6 servings.*

# Cheese Strata

12 slices of day-
    old bread
½ pound process
    Cheddar cheese,
    thinly sliced
4 eggs
2½ cups milk

½ teaspoon prepared
    mustard
1 tablespoon minced
    onion
1 teaspoon salt
Dash Tabasco
    sauce

Trim crusts from bread. Arrange 6 bread slices in greased baking dish 12" x 8" x 2"; cover with cheese slices, then with remaining bread slices. Beat eggs; blend in milk and remaining ingredients; pour over bread. Chill 1 hour. Bake, uncovered, at 325° about 50 minutes, or until puffy and brown. Serve at once. *Makes 6 servings.*

# Chicken - Cheese Fondue

4 eggs, separated
2 cups small, fresh
  bread cubes
1 cup grated process
  sharp Cheddar
  cheese

1 can (10½ ounces)
  condensed cream-
  of-chicken soup,
  undiluted

Beat egg whites until stiff but not dry. Beat yolks until thick and lemon-colored; add bread cubes, cheese and soup, mix well. Fold gently into stiffly beaten egg whites; turn into 1½-quart greased casserole. Bake at 325° for 1 hour, or until knife, inserted in center, comes out clean. Serve at once. *Makes 6 servings.*

# Crabmeat Fondue

1 can (6½ ounces)
  crabmeat
1 cup finely diced
  celery
¼ cup mayonnaise
1 tablespoon pre-
  pared mustard
¼ teaspoon salt
12 thin slices whole
  wheat bread

¾ pound sharp
  Cheddar cheese,
  sliced thin
2 eggs
1½ cups milk
2 teaspoons Wor-
  cestershire sauce

Combine crabmeat and celery. Blend mayonnaise, mustard and salt; add to crabmeat mixture; mix well. Spread between bread slices. Cut sandwiches in half. Arrange sandwiches and cheese slices in greased casserole in alternate layers. Beat eggs; add milk and Worcestershire sauce. Pour into casserole. Bake at 325° for 45 minutes. Serve immediately. *Makes 6 servings.*

# Ham And Cheese Fondue

12 slices white bread
3 cans (2 ¼ ounces each) deviled ham
1 cup shredded Cheddar cheese
4 eggs, slightly beaten
2 cups milk
Dash Tabasco sauce
1 teaspoon salt

Trim crusts from bread. Spread 6 slices with deviled ham; top with remaining 6 slices. Cut sandwiches into quarters. Place sandwiches in single layer in greased 9-inch square pan. Sprinkle with cheese. Combine eggs, milk, Tabasco and salt. Pour milk mixture over sandwiches. Bake at 350° for 25 to 30 minutes or until a knife inserted near edge comes out clean. *Makes 6 servings.*

# Vegetable Cheese Fondue

1 cup milk
1 cup soft bread crumbs
1 tablespoon butter or margarine
½ teaspoon salt
Few grains paprika
Few grains pepper
¼ pound sharp Cheddar cheese, grated
3 eggs, separated
1 cup cooked green peas

Scald milk; combine with crumbs, butter or margarine, salt, paprika and pepper. Add cheese. Add unbeaten egg yolks; mix well. Add peas. Beat egg whites stiff; fold in. Bake in greased casserole at 350° for 45 minutes. Serve at once. *Makes 4 generous servings.*

*Note:* Any cooked vegetable may be used instead of peas.

24

# Fondue Provencale

1 ½ long loaves French bread
½ cup butter or margarine
½ cup sharp prepared mustard
1 ½ pounds sharp Cheddar cheese, sliced ¼-inch thick
4 eggs, well beaten
5 cups hot milk
1 ½ teaspoons Worcestershire sauce
1 teaspoon salt
Dash Tabasco sauce
¼ teaspoon paprika

Slice French bread into ½-inch slices; spread generously with butter and mustard. Let stand several hours or overnight. Alternate layers of bread and cheese slices to fill 4-quart casserole. Combine eggs, milk, Worcestershire, salt and Tabasco. Pour over bread and cheese. Sprinkle top with paprika. Chill several hours or over-night. Bake, uncovered, at 350° for 1 ½ hours. *Makes 8 servings.*

# 3.
# Rabbits
# And Their Relatives

Rabbits (sometimes called rarebits) are close relatives of fondues, and *they* have relatives called by strange names such as English Monkey, White Monkey, Rum Tum Tiddy, Woodchuck and so on.

The recipes that follow are easy to prepare, in a skillet, chafing dish or electric fry pan. They make wonderful main dishes for a kitchen party, a teen-age get together, a Sunday night supper or any informal occasion. Just add a salad, a simple dessert and a beverage to round out the meal.

# Caraway Welsh Rabbit

1 teaspoon dry
mustard
¾ cup evaporated
milk
1 pound Cheddar
cheese, shredded

2 teaspoons Wor-
cestershire sauce
1 teaspoon salt
1 teaspoon caraway
seed

Blend mustard with milk in top of double boiler.
Add remaining ingredients. Cook over boiling water,
stirring often, until cheese is melted and ingredients
are well blended. Serve on rusks. *Makes 6 servings.*


# Classic Welsh Rabbit

¼ cup butter or
margarine
2 tablespoons flour
1 cup stale ale or
beer
2 teaspoons dry
mustard
Dash of cayenne

¼ teaspoon paprika
2 teaspoons Wor-
cestershire sauce
8 cups (2 pounds)
grated sharp
Cheddar cheese
4 whole eggs,
slightly beaten

Melt butter in top of double boiler. Stir in flour;
blend well. Add ale or beer slowly. Cook, stirring
constantly, until sauce thickens. Add mustard, cayenne, paprika and Worcestershire sauce. Mix well.
Add grated cheese; continue to cook until cheese
melts, stirring occasionally. Add a little of the hot
mixture to the eggs; slowly stir egg mixture into
cheese mixture. Serve immediately over hot toasted
crackers or hot thin toast. *Makes 8 servings.*

# Fluffy Tomato Rabbit

1 can (10¾ ounces)
   condensed tomato
   soup
½ cup water
½ cup thinly
   sliced onions
1 pound Cheddar
   cheese, thinly
   sliced

2 eggs, separated
1 teaspoon Wor-
   cestershire sauce
1 teaspoon dry
   mustard
1 teaspoon salt
Dash Tabasco sauce
Rusks

Combine soup and water; bring to boil; remove from heat. Add onions; cook until soft but not brown. Add cheese; stir until melted. Combine egg yolks, Worcestershire sauce and seasonings; beat well; stir into cheese mixture. Cook and stir over low heat 2 minutes. Beat egg whites stiff but not dry; fold in. Serve on rusks. *Makes 4 servings.*

# Crabmeat Rabbit

½ cup butter or
   margarine
½ cup dry white
   wine
1 pound American
   cheese, cubed
1 teaspoon Wor-
   cestershire sauce

Dash Tabasco sauce
1 can (6½ ounces)
   crabmeat, drained
   and flaked
Buttered toast
   points

Melt butter over hot water in chafing dish. Stir in wine. Add cheese in small amounts, stirring until melted. Blend in Worcestershire sauce, Tabasco and crabmeat. Serve over toast points. *Makes 4 to 6 servings.*

# Chili Rabbit

½ cup light cream
½ cup canned con-
  densed consommé,
  undiluted
1 pound sliced
  process sharp
  cheese

1 can (1 pound)
  chili con carne
Corn crisps

Add light cream, consommé and cheese to chili con carne in blazer of chafing dish over direct heat. Cook, stirring occasionally, until cheese melts. Blend well. Serve over corn crisps. *Makes 6 servings.*

# Mexican Rabbit

2 tablespoons
  butter or mar-
  garine
1 small onion,
  minced
2 tablespoons chopped
  green pepper
2 cups grated
  American cheese
1 can (1 pound)
  whole kernel corn

1 egg, well beaten
½ cup hot, canned
  tomatoes
½ cup soft bread
  crumbs
½ teaspoon salt
¼ teaspoon chili
  powder (or to
  taste)

Melt butter in double boiler. Add onion and green pepper; cook until onion is soft. Add cheese; stir until melted; add corn mixed with egg. Add remaining ingredients; heat thoroughly. Serve over toast garnished with crisp slices of bacon. *Makes 6 servings.*

# Ham And Cheese Rabbit

¼  cup butter or
    margarine
¼  cup all-purpose
    flour
1 ¼  cups milk
¾  cup tomato juice

2  cups grated sharp
   Cheddar cheese
1  large can (4 ½
   ounces) deviled
   ham
Toast

Melt butter in blazer pan of chafing dish over direct heat. Remove from heat. Stir in flour to make smooth paste. Stir in milk gradually until smooth. Return to heat; bring to boiling, stirring constantly. Boil, stirring constantly, 5 minutes, or until thickened. Stir in tomato juice; cook 5 minutes longer. Add cheese and ham; cook, stirring occasionally, 5 minutes longer. Remove blazer pan from direct heat; place over boiling water in water pan. Serve over toast. *Makes 4 to 6 servings.*

# Mock Welsh Rabbit

3  cups grated
   Cheddar cheese
½  teaspoon dry
   mustard

1  cup thin
   white sauce

Add cheese and mustard to hot white sauce; stir over very low heat until cheese is melted and mixture is smooth. *Makes 4 to 6 servings.*

***Tomato Rabbit:***

Substitute 1 can condensed tomato soup ( 1 ⅓ cups) for white sauce.

# Oyster Rabbit

1 pint oysters
2 tablespoons butter
  or margarine
¼ pound Swiss
  cheese, diced
½ teaspoon salt

Dash Tabasco
  sauce
2 eggs, beaten
2 tablespoons dry
  sherry
Toast

Cook oysters in their liquor until edges curl. Drain; save liquor. Combine butter, cheese, salt and Tabasco in top of double boiler. Cook and stir until cheese melts and mixture is smooth. Stir in oyster liquor. If necessary add a little light cream to make sauce the right consistency. Pour a little of the hot mixture on eggs; return to remaining hot mixture. Add oysters and sherry. Heat to serving temperature. Serve on toast sprinkled with paprika or chopped parsley. *Makes 4 servings.*

# Quick Rabbit

½ pound process
  Cheddar cheese
1 can (8 ounces)
  tomato sauce

2 teaspoons minced
  onion
4 to 5 drops Tabasco sauce

Slice cheese into chafing dish or double boiler. When cheese is melted stir in tomato sauce, onion and Tabasco; heat thoroughly. Serve on toasted English muffins. *Makes 3 or 4 servings.*

# Shrimp Rabbit

½ cup diced green pepper

¼ cup butter or margarine

¼ cup flour

2 cups milk

4 slices American pasteurized processed cheese, cut in strips

1 teaspoon Worcestershire sauce

¼ teaspoon dry mustard

¼ teaspoon paprika

Dash of Tabasco sauce

1 can (5 ½ ounces) shrimp

4 English muffins, toasted

Cook green pepper in butter or margarine until tender; blend in flour. Add milk gradually; stir until thickened. Add cheese, Worcestershire sauce, mustard, paprika and Tabasco; stir until cheese is melted. Add shrimp; heat. Serve on English muffins. *Makes 4 servings.*

# Tomato-Mushroom Rabbit

4 tablespoons butter or margarine, divided

2 tablespoons flour

¾ cup milk

1 can (10¾ ounces) condensed tomato soup

1 can (4 ounces) mushroom crowns

2 eggs

1 ¾ cups cubed mild American cheese

Few grains salt

Toast

Melt 2 tablespoons butter or margarine in top of double boiler. Blend in flour. Combine milk and soup; add. Cook over hot water, stirring constantly, until thick. Cut mushrooms in half; sauté in remaining butter or margarine until delicate brown. Beat eggs slightly. Add soup mixture to beaten eggs.

Add mushrooms, cheese and salt. Heat slowly, stirring often, until cheese melts. Serve on toast. *Makes 4 servings.*

## Ripe Olive Rabbit

2 tablespoons butter or margarine
2 tablespoons flour
1 cup sauterne
4 cups grated process American cheese
¾ teaspoon dry mustard
½ mashed garlic clove
½ teaspoon Worcestershire sauce
Dash Tabasco sauce
1 cup quartered pitted ripe olives
12 slices pumpernickel bread

Melt butter in double boiler; blend in flour. Add sauterne and cheese; stir until cheese is melted. Add mustard, garlic, Worcestershire, Tabasco and ripe olives. Cut each pumpernickel slice into 2 triangles. Pour cheese mixture over pumpernickel triangles. *Makes 4 servings.*

## Royal Rabbit

¼ cup butter or margarine
¼ cup flour
1 ½ cups milk
Dash Tabasco sauce
Dash dry mustard
1 stick (10 ounces) Cheddar club cheese, crumbled
6 tomato slices
6 slices white bread, toasted

Make a white sauce with butter or margarine, flour, milk and seasonings. Add cheese; stir until melted. For each serving, spoon sauce over sliced tomato on toast. *Makes 6 servings.*

# Tuna Rabbit

2 tablespoons butter or margarine
2 tablespoons flour
1 teaspoon dry mustard
2 cups milk
2 eggs
½ pound American cheese, grated
1 teaspoon salt
2 teaspoons Worcestershire sauce
2 cans (6 ½ or 7 ounces each) tuna

Melt butter or margarine; add flour and mustard; blend well. Add milk; cook over hot water, stirring constantly, until thickened. Beat eggs. Pour hot milk mixture on eggs. Return to double boiler; add cheese, salt and Worcestershire sauce. Cook, stirring, until cheese melts. Drain tuna; flake; add. Heat thoroughly. *Makes 6 servings.*

# Turkey-Cheese Rabbit

½ cup dry sherry
2 tablespoons minced onion
½ cup diced green pepper
1 cup grated process American cheese
2 tablespoons flour
1 teaspoon salt
1 cup evaporated milk
1 can (6 ounces) broiled mushroom crowns
Left-over turkey, sliced or cubed

Combine all ingredients except mushrooms and turkey in top of double boiler; add liquid from mushrooms. Stir over hot water until cheese melts and mixture thickens. Add mushrooms. If there is enough turkey to slice serve sauce separately. If not, cube and add to sauce. *Makes enough sauce for 6 to 8 servings.*

34

# Tomato Rabbit on Eggs

2 tablespoons grated onion
2 tablespoons butter or margarine
1 can (10¾ ounces) condensed tomato soup
1½ cups grated sharp Cheddar cheese
1 egg, beaten
1 teaspoon Worchestershire sauce
Salt and paprika to taste
Dash Tabasco sauce
4 hard-cooked eggs, sliced
4 slices hot, buttered toast

Cook onion in butter for 2 minutes. Add soup; heat. Stir in cheese; cook and stir until cheese is melted. Pour a little of the tomato mixture on beaten egg; return to remaining tomato mixture. Stir in Worcestershire sauce and seasonings. Cook 2 minutes, stirring. Arrange egg slices on toast. Top with rabbit. *Makes 4 servings.*

# Beef Salmagundi

¼ pound dried beef, shredded
3 tablespoons butter or margarine
1 cup diced onions
2 tablespoons flour
2 cups cooked or canned tomatoes
1½ cups cooked kidney beans
½ to ¾ teaspoon chili powder
Cornbread squares

Cook dried beef with butter in heavy skillet until edges curl. Add onions; cook about 5 minutes longer. Stir in flour, blending it with the fat in skillet. Stir in tomatoes. Cook over low heat, stirring constantly, until thick. Add beans and chili powder. Simmer 5 minutes. Serve on cornbread squares. *Makes 4 to 6 servings.*

# Cheese Ditty

2 cups grated process American cheese
1 can (10¾ ounces) condensed tomato soup
1 tablespoon minced onion
1 tablespoon catchup
¼ teaspoon dry mustard
¼ teaspoon salt
Dash Tabasco sauce
1 egg, beaten
4 slices toast

Melt cheese in double boiler. Heat soup with onion, catchup, mustard, salt and Tabasco; add to cheese with beaten egg. Cook 5 minutes, stirring constantly. Serve on crisp toast. *Makes 4 servings.*

# English Monkey

1 cup stale bread crumbs
1 cup milk
1 tablespoon butter or margarine
½ cup soft mild cheese, cut in small pieces
1 egg, slightly beaten
½ teaspoon salt
Few grains cayenne

Soak bread crumbs for 15 minutes in milk. Melt butter; add cheese. When cheese has melted, add soaked crumbs, egg and seasonings. Cook three minutes; pour over toast or toasted crackers which have been lightly buttered.

# Rum Tum Tiddy

1 can (10¾ ounces) condensed tomato soup
½ pound quick-melting process cheese
½ teaspoon dry mustard
4 slices toast
4 slices crisp bacon

36

Combine all ingredients except bacon. Cook and stir until cheese is melted. Serve over toast with crumbled bacon on top. *Makes 4 servings.*

## White Monkey

2 cups soft day-old bread crumbs
2 cups milk
4 cups grated process American Cheddar cheese
2 teaspoons bottled thick meat sauce

½ teaspoon dry mustard
¾ teaspoon salt
Dash Tabasco sauce
6 slices toast

Soak bread crumbs and milk in top of double boiler 5 minutes. Add cheese and next 4 ingredients. Cook over boiling water, stirring, until cheese is melted. Serve on toast. *Makes 6 servings.*

## Woodchuck

2 cups grated sharp Cheddar cheese
1 can (10¾ ounces) condensed tomato soup
3 tablespoons water

½ teaspoon salt
Dash Tabasco sauce
Toast or toasted crackers

Melt cheese over low heat, stirring often. Add soup, water, salt and Tabasco. Mix well. Heat to serving temperature. Serve on toast or toasted crackers. *Makes 4 servings.*

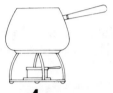

# 4.
# Fondues
# Bourguignonnes

IT ALL started with Beef Fondue Bourguignonne. The name is a complete mystery because nothing is melted (fondue is said to be derived from the French verb, fondre, to melt) and no red wine from Burgundy is used in preparing it! All this has not interfered with its popularity as a party dish, even though special equipment is needed and specific rules must be followed.

Beef Fondue Bourguignonne is far and away the most popular version. Tender beef is cut in bite-size chunks, speared on fondue forks and dunked in fat hot enough to bubble. We recommend vegetable oil or a combination of vegetable oil and clarified butter. The beef is held in the fat just long enough to cook it to the desired degree of doneness (see recipe for Classic Beef Fondue Bourguignonne). Then it is

38

dunked in a sauce chosen from a group of four or so (see Chapter 5). As is the case with Cheese Fondue, only four or five people should be at one table or forks may tangle.

It is best to supply each participant with *two* forks, one fondue fork for dunking and one regular fork for eating, and a small plate to hold chunks of beef and spoonfuls of sauces (or use compartmented dishes especially designed for this use). Supply paper napkins in abundance and fingerbowls of warm water garnished with a lemon or lime slice or a mint sprig. Always use a washable tablecloth—plastic is ideal— so you won't grieve over spatters or spills which are sure to occur.

Unless you are using a specially designed heat-controlled electric fondue pot, heat the oil (or oil and clarified butter*) over direct heat until it is almost smoking hot, transfer to the fondue pot and set it over a warmer. This fondue pot is smaller than the one used for cheese fondue and is made of metal with a base broader than the top. Don't fill it more than half full. Control the heat so that the fat bubbles but does not smoke.

*To clarify butter: melt butter over hot water. Remove from heat. When milk solids have settled to the bottom, strain the clear butter through a very fine sieve or cheesecloth into a jar. Cover tightly. This may be stored in the refrigerator for about three weeks.

## OTHER TYPES OF FONDUES BOURGUIGNONNES

Meats other than beef may be prepared and cooked in this way. Chicken, pork, lamb, fish and shellfish are delicious as fondues.

The menus that follow point up the use of Fondues Bourguignonnes as party fare, suggest foods to precede and follow the dunking session and provide recipes for these dishes.

# A NET-FULL OF FISH AND SHELLFISH FONDUES

## Swordfish Fondue

Swordfish, firm-fleshed and boneless, is ideal for fondue cooking. Select steaks about 1-inch thick and cut into cubes. Spear cubes on fondue fork and cook briefly as directed for Classic Beef Fondue, p. 44. The fish will lose its transparent look when done. Serve with a choice of sauces suggested for fish and shellfish in Chapter 5.

## Rock Lobster Fondue

Cut shelled rock lobster tails into slices about 1-inch thick. Spear slices on fondue fork and cook briefly as directed for Classic Beef Fondue, p. 44. Serve with a choice of sauces suggested for fish and shellfish in Chapter 5.

## Shrimp Fondue

Peel and devein shrimp, allowing at least ¼ pound per person. Spear shrimp on fondue forks and cook briefly as directed for Classic Beef Fondue, p. 44. Serve with a choice of sauces suggested for fish and shellfish in Chapter 5.

## Scallop Fondue

Use sea scallops, allowing at least ¼ pound per person. Spear scallops on fondue forks and cook briefly as directed for Classic Beef Fondue, p. 44. Serve with a choice of sauces suggested for fish and shellfish in **Chapter** 5.

# CONTINENTAL PARTY

Beef Fondue Tyrolean*
Dutch Salad*
French Bread
Viennese Chocolate Cherry Kuchen*
Coffee

## Beef Fondue Tyrolean

| | | | |
|---|---|---|---|
| 1 | can (10½ ounces) beef broth | ½ | teaspoon salt |
| 1½ | cups white wine | ½ | teaspoon cracked pepper |
| 1 | onion, thinly sliced | ½ | teaspoon thyme |
| 1 | garlic clove, halved | ½ | teaspoon tarragon |
| 1 | cup coarsely chopped celery and celery tops | 2 | pounds lean top sirloin |
| 3 | sprigs parsley | | Horseradish Sauce, Mustard Mayonnaise, Sweet Sour Sauce (see below) |
| 1 | whole clove | | |

Combine all ingredients except beef and sauces; bring to a boil; lower heat; simmer 5 minutes. Cover; let stand 2 hours. Strain. Heat to boiling in fondue pot. Trim fat from beef and cut into bite-size cubes. Spear beef with fondue forks. Cook in hot broth 1½ to 2 minutes. (The broth may be used for soup after the meat is cooked.) Serve with sauces. *Makes 4 servings.*

### *Horseradish Sauce:*
Combine 1 cup dairy sour cream, 1 teaspoon prepared horseradish, 1 tablespoon chopped chives and ¾ teaspoon seasoned salt.

### Mustard Mayonnaise:

Combine ¾ cup mayonnaise, 1 tablespoon chopped green onion, 1 teaspoon prepared mustard and 1 drop Tabasco sauce.

### Sweet Sour Sauce:

Combine 1 cup catchup, 3 tablespoons wine vinegar, 1 teaspoon sugar and a dash salt.

## Dutch Salad

| | |
|---|---|
| ⅔ cup seedless raisins | 4 tablespoons chopped green onion |
| 4 ½ cups shredded crisp cabbage | 3 cups cubed apples |

Rinse raisins; drain. Combine with cabbage, onion and apples. Serve on lettuce with the following dressing:

| | |
|---|---|
| ⅓ cup cider vinegar | Pepper to taste |
| ⅓ cup sugar | 1 tablespoon corn-starch |
| ½ teaspoon salt | ⅓ cup cold water |
| ⅓ cup vegetable oil | 1 egg |

Combine vinegar, sugar, salt, oil and pepper. Dissolve cornstarch in cold water; add. Bring to boil; continue cooking and stirring until mixture thickens and is clear (about 3 to 4 minutes). Remove from heat. Beat egg. Pour hot mixture slowly on egg, beating constantly; continue beating until mixture is thick; cool. *Makes 6 servings.*

# Viennese Chocolate Cherry Kuchen

1 ½ cups butter
  6 squares (6 ounces) unsweetened chocolate
  3 cups sugar
  6 eggs, beaten
  3 cups sifted cake flour
  ¾ teaspoon baking powder
  ¾ teaspoon salt
  1 can (1 pound) pitted sour red cherries
  1 tablespoon vanilla

Melt butter and chocolate together over hot water. Add sugar to beaten eggs gradually, while beating. Add chocolate mixture to egg mixture; beat hard for 1 minute. Mix and sift flour, baking powder, and salt. Drain cherries thoroughly; add to flour mixture; stir into chocolate-egg mixture. Stir in vanilla. Divide batter evenly among three greased and floured 10-inch layer-cake pans. Bake at 350° for 30 to 40 minutes. When cool, put together with sweetened whipped cream. Garnish top with whipped cream. Chill.

● ● ●

# ELECTION NIGHT SUPPER

California Green Goddess Salad*
Classic Beef Fondue Bourguignonne*
Garlic Bread
Assorted Dips and Sauces
Pumpkin Pie
Coffee

# California Green Goddess Salad

| | |
|---|---|
| 1 garlic clove, grated | 2 tablespoons tarragon wine vinegar |
| 1 can (2 ounces) anchovy fillets, finely chopped | ½ cup dairy sour cream |
| ¼ cup chopped chives, fresh or freeze-dried | 1 cup mayonnaise |
| | ¼ cup minced parsley |
| 1 tablespoon lemon juice | Salt and coarse black pepper, to taste |

Combine all ingredients in order given. Pour over coarsely torn mixed greens. Toss well. *Makes about 2 cups of dressing.*

# Classic Beef Fondue Bourguignonne

| | |
|---|---|
| 2 pounds beef tenderloin or top sirloin cut in ¾-inch cubes | Dipping sauces Hot, sliced garlic bread |
| Vegetable oil or buttery flavor oil | |

Trim off fat and connective tissue before cubing beef. Arrange on platter. Oil in fondue pot should be about 2-inches deep, heated to 400°. Spear beef cube on fondue fork and cook in the bubbling oil to desired degree of doneness. This depends on size of beef cube and temperature of oil, but, as a guide, cook about ½ minute for rare, 50 seconds for medium-well and 1 to 1½ minutes for well-done. Transfer to a cool fork, dip in desired sauce. *Makes 5 to 6 servings.*

# THANKSGIVING WEEKEND BRUNCH

Cream of Mushroom Soup
Chicken or Turkey Fondue*
Assorted Dips and Sauces
Creamy Tomato Aspic Salad*
Hot Buttered Rolls
Burnt Almond Cake*
Coffee

## Chicken or Turkey Fondue

Cut boned breast meat into bite-size pieces. Spear on
fondue forks and cook as directed for Classic Beef
Fondue, p. 44. Offer a choice of sauces.

## Creamy Tomato Aspic Salad

2 tablespoons un-
  flavored gelatin
½ cup cold water
2 cans (8 ounces each)
  tomato sauce
2 tablespoons lemon
  juice
1 cup dairy sour
  cream
½ cup Rhine wine

½ teaspoon salt
1 tablespoon instant
  minced onion
3 tablespoons cold
  water
2 tablespoons
  minced parsley
1 cup thinly sliced
  celery

Soften gelatin in ½ cup cold water. Heat tomato
sauce to boiling; add to gelatin; stir until dissolved.
Add lemon juice, sour cream, wine and salt. Chill
until slightly thickened. Meanwhile, combine instant
minced onion and 3 tablespoons cold water; let
stand until water is absorbed. Fold into thickened
gelatin with parsley and celery. Spoon into 5-cup
mold; chill until set. Unmold on serving plate. Garnish with stuffed olives and sprigs of watercress.
*Makes 6 to 8 servings.*

# Burnt Almond Cake

½ cup white short-
  ening
1 cup sugar
3 egg whites
½ teaspoon almond
  extract

2 cups sifted all-
  purpose flour
3 teaspoons baking
  powder
¼ teaspoon salt
⅔ cup milk

Cream shortening to consistency of mayonnaise; add sugar. Add unbeaten egg whites, one at a time, beating well after each addition. Add almond extract. Mix and sift flour, baking powder and salt. Add alternately with milk to first mixture. Bake in 2 greased 9-inch cake pans at 375° for 25 to 30 minutes. Cool on cake rack.

## *Frosting:*

1 ½ cups blanched
    almonds
  1 cup butter or
    margarine
2 ⅔ cups confectioners'
    (powdered)
    sugar

Hot milk or
  cream
½ teaspoon almond
  extract

Put almonds in shallow pan with about 2 table-spoons vegetable oil. Place in hot oven, 450°. Stir often until almonds are deep golden brown. Drain on absorbent paper. Crush quite fine with rolling pin. Cream butter or margarine. Add sugar gradually, with enough hot milk to make good spreading consistency. Add flavoring. Put cake layers together with frosting. Frost top and sides. Cover entire cake with almonds, pressing into frosting.

# AFTER WINTER-SPORTS PARTY

Green Pea Soup
Croutons
Pork Fondue*
Assorted Dips and Sauces
Buttered Baking Powder Biscuits
Fruit Dessert Salad
Fruit Salad Dressing*
Coffee

## Pork Fondue

Cut lean boneless pork into bite-size pieces. Cook as directed for Classic Beef Fondue, p. 44, but be sure pork is completely cooked through. Offer a choice of sauces.

## Fruit Salad Dressing

| | |
|---|---|
| 1  tablespoon flour | Juice of ½ lemon |
| ⅓  cup sugar | Juice of ½ large |
| 1  egg, well-beaten | orange |
| ½  cup canned | ½  cup whipping |
| pineapple juice | cream |

Mix flour and sugar in top of small double boiler. Add egg and strained fruit juices; blend. Cook over hot water, stirring constantly until thick. Cool. Whip cream; fold in. *Makes 6 servings.*

# HOUSE PAINTING PARTY

Sausage Fondue*
Assorted Dips and Dunks
Perfection Salad*
Party Rye Bread and Butter Sandwiches
Apple Cake*
Coffee

## Sausage Fondue

Cut frankfurters into bite-size pieces, or use whole cocktail weiners, Vienna sausages, cocktail smokies or any other small, ready-to-eat sausages. Cook as directed for Classic Beef Fondue, p. 44, just until browned and hot. Offer a choice of sauces.

## Perfection Salad

| | |
|---|---|
| 1 envelope (1 table-spoon) unflavored gelatin | ¼ cup vinegar |
| | 1 cup shredded raw cabbage |
| 2 tablespoons cold water | ¾ cup diced celery |
| 1 cup boiling water | 1 tablespoon minced green pepper |
| 2 tablespoons sugar | ¼ cup minced pimiento |
| 1 teaspoon salt | |
| Few grains pepper | Lettuce |
| ¾ cup sweetened grapefruit juice | Mayonnaise or salad dressing |

Sprinkle gelatin on cold water. Dissolve in boiling water. Add sugar, salt, pepper, grapefruit juice and vinegar. Stir until sugar dissolves. Chill until syrupy. Fold in cabbage, celery, green pepper and pimiento. Turn into 6 individual molds which have been rinsed in cold water. Chill until firm. Unmold on lettuce. Garnish with mayonnaise or salad dressing. *Makes 6 servings.*

## Apple Cake

2 cups biscuit mix
⅓ cup sugar
2 eggs, slightly beaten
½ cup heavy cream
3 cups (approximately) thinly sliced apples
1 teaspoon cinnamon
¼ teaspoon allspice
¼ teaspoon nutmeg
¼ cup sugar
¼ cup melted butter or margarine

Combine biscuit mix and ⅓ cup sugar. Combine eggs and cream; stir into biscuit mix with fork. Spread dough in bottom of greased 8-inch spring form pan. Arrange apple slices on top, pressing cut edges slightly into dough. Combine spices and ¼ cup sugar; sprinkle over apples. Pour melted butter evenly over all. Cover top with foil. Bake at 400° for 15 minutes. Remove foil; bake 20 minutes longer or until apples are tender and dough tests done. Remove from pan. Serve warm, cut into wedges, with lemon sauce or hard sauce. *Makes 6 to 8 servings.*

## ST. PATRICK'S DAY SUPPER

Lamb Fondue*
Assorted Dips and Sauces
Emerald Isle Salad*
Irish Soda Bread*   Potato Chips
Fruited Lime Gelatin

# Lamb Fondue

Cut boneless lean lamb into bite-size chunks. Cook as directed for Classic Beef Fondue, p. 44. Offer a choice of sauces.

## Emerald Isle Salad

| | |
|---|---|
| 1 can (1 pound) green beans | 2 cups shredded uncooked spinach |
| French dressing, bottled or home-made | ½ teaspoon curry powder |
| 1 small head lettuce | 1 avocado, diced or sliced |

Drain liquid from can of green beans and fill can with French dressing. Return green beans to the refrigerator to marinate 2 hours. Wash greens well; drain; refrigerate. When chilled and crisp, tear lettuce and spinach into small pieces. Drain green beans, saving the dressing. Shake curry powder into dressing. Add green beans and avocado to the salad; toss, using only enough of the dressing to moisten. *Makes 6 servings.*

## Irish Soda Bread

| | |
|---|---|
| 4 cups sifted all-purpose flour | 1 to 1 ½ cups seedless raisins |
| ¼ cup sugar | 1 ⅓ cups buttermilk |
| 1 teaspoon salt | 1 egg |
| 1 teaspoon baking powder | 1 teaspoon baking soda |
| ¼ cup butter or margarine | |

Mix and sift flour, sugar, salt and baking powder. Cut in butter or margarine with pastry blender or two knives until mixture resembles coarse corn meal. Stir in raisins. Combine buttermilk, egg and baking soda. Stir buttermilk mixture into flour mixture until just moistened. Bake in greased 1 or 1½ quart pudding pan or casserole at 375° for 45 to 50 minutes or until golden brown.

## EASTER BRUNCH

Ham Fondue*
Assorted Dips and Sauces
Garden Relish Salad*    Deviled Eggs
Hot Buttered Finger Rolls
Easter Dessert Ring*

## Ham Fondue

Cut ready-to-eat ham into bite-size chunks. Cook as directed for Classic Beef Fondue, p. 44, just until browned and heated through. Offer a choice of sauces.

## Garden Relish Salad

1 package lemon-
  flavored gelatin
2 cups water
1 teaspoon salt
1 teaspoon vinegar
1 cup diced
  cucumber

1 cup sliced
  radishes
½ cup sliced spring
  onions (scallions)
Water cress

Dissolve gelatin in water as directed on package. Add salt and vinegar. Chill until slightly thicker than unbeaten egg white. Fold in cucumber, radishes and onions. Spoon into 5-cup ring mold. Chill until set. Unmold. Garnish with water cress. *Makes 6 servings.*

## Easter Dessert Ring

½ cup sugar
½ teaspoon salt
1 cup light corn syrup
4 teaspoons butter or margarine
5 cups cornflakes

1 cup salted peanuts
3 pints assorted ice cream
Chocolate Sauce (see below)

Combine sugar and salt; add corn syrup slowly, stirring to blend. Cook over low heat, stirring occasionally, to 242°, or until a little forms a soft ball when dropped in cold water. Remove from heat; add butter or margarine; pour over cornflakes and peanuts; toss lightly with a fork until well blended. When cool enough to handle, shape in a ring on serving plate. Fill with egg-shaped scoops of assorted ice cream. Serve with chocolate sauce. *Makes 8 servings.*

### *Chocolate Sauce:*

2 squares unsweetened chocolate

¾ cup light corn syrup
1 teaspoon vanilla

Melt chocolate over hot water; blend in corn syrup. Add vanilla. *Makes about 1 cup.*

# SEASHORE PARTY

Clam Chowder
Pilot Crackers
Mixed Seafood Fondue*
Assorted Dips, Sauces, Relishes
Old Fashioned Cole Slaw*
Lemon Chiffon Crunch*

## Mixed Seafood Fondue

Arrange shrimp, scallops, rock lobster tail slices and swordfish cubes (or cubes of any firm-fleshed fish), attractively garnished, on separate platters or on a large chop plate so that guests may make their own selection. Offer a choice of sauces. Cook briefly as directed for Classic Beef Fondue, p. 44.

## Old Fashioned Cole Slaw

⅓ cup sugar
½ teaspoon dry mustard
¼ teaspoon salt
Few grains pepper
1 egg
⅓ cup milk

⅓ cup vinegar
1 tablespoon butter or margarine
3 cups shredded cabbage
Paprika

Combine sugar, mustard, salt and pepper. Beat egg; add. Add milk; mix well. Add vinegar slowly. Cook, stirring constantly until mixture boils. Add butter or margarine; stir until melted. Chill. Toss dressing with shredded cabbage; sprinkle with paprika. *Makes 4 servings.*

# Lemon Chiffon Crunch

1 ½ cups graham
    cracker crumbs
⅓ cup light brown
    sugar
½ teaspoon cinnamon
⅓ cup melted butter
    or margarine
1 package lemon-
    flavored gelatin

¾ cup boiling
    water
½ cup sugar
Juice and grated
    peel of 1 lemon
1 tall can (1 ⅔ cups)
    evaporated milk

Combine crumbs, brown sugar, cinnamon and melted butter; mix until crumbly. Reserve 3 tablespoons; press remainder in bottom of buttered 9-inch square pan; chill. Dissolve gelatin in boiling water; add sugar, lemon juice and peel. Chill to consistency of unbeaten egg whites. Pour evaporated milk into freezer tray; freeze until ice crystals form around edges; turn into chilled bowl; whip until stiff. Fold whipped evaporated milk into gelatin mixture; spoon into pan on top of crumb layer. Sprinkle top with reserved crumb mixture. Chill until set. *Cut into 12 squares to serve.*

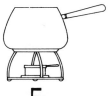

# 5.
# Sauces,
# Dips And Relishes

When you are serving Beef Fondue Bourguignonne or a fondue featuring other kinds of meat, poultry, fish or shellfish, it is very important to select at least four sauces, dips or relishes as accompaniments. This should be easy, with fifty or so to choose from on the following pages, but to make it easier still, here is a list indicating "which goes with which."

***Beef:***
Bearnaise, horseradish, creole, cumberland, curry, Mexicana, fluffy mustard, mustard mayonnaise, piquante, sour cream, steak, barbecue.

### Lamb:
Savory cream, horseradish, creole, cumberland, dill, currant-orange, curry, Mexicana, mint, golden mint, barbecue.

### Pork:
Raw apple relish, anchovy, savory cream, creole, whole cranberry, cranberry and horseradish relish, currant-orange, curry, Mexicana, peanut curry, barbecue.

### Ham:
Raw apple relish, horseradish, whole cranberry, cranberry and horseradish relish, fluffy mustard, mustard mayonnaise, peanut curry, barbecue.

### Poultry:
Raw apple relish, anchovy, creole, cumberland, whole cranberry, cranberry and horseradish relish, currant-orange, curry, Mexicana, sweet sour, tarragon caper, mornay, soubise, barbecue.

### Fish or Shellfish:
Anchovy, butter, cocktail, caper, creole, drawn butter, curry, garden dressing, Hollandaise, Louis, Mexicana, fluffy mustard, mustard mayonnaise, savory green, seafood, quick shrimp, tartar, tarragon caper, vert, vinegar, mousseline, remoulade (shrimp), soubise, sea goddess, hot wine mayonnaise.

### Vegetables:
Butter, curry, Hollandaise, mornay, never-fail Hollandaise, hot wine mayonnaise.

# Anchovy Sauce

2 teaspoons anchovy paste

1 cup melted butter or margarine
⅓ cup dry sherry

Blend anchovy paste with melted butter. Stir in sherry. Heat to boiling point; simmer 5 minutes, or until sauce thickens slightly, stirring vigorously. *Makes about 1⅓ cups.*

# Barbecue Sauce

2 cans (8 ounces each) tomato sauce
2 tablespoons Worcestershire sauce
1 tablespoon prepared horseradish
Dash Tabasco sauce

1 tablespoon sugar
1 tablespoon grated onion
½ teaspoon oregano
⅛ teaspoon cloves
2 tablespoons butter or margarine

Combine all ingredients; stir over low heat until butter melts. *Makes about 2⅓ cups.*

# Butter Sauce

¼ cup butter
2 tablespoons flour
½ teaspoon salt

⅛ teaspoon paprika
Dash Tabasco sauce
1 cup water

Melt butter in saucepan. Blend in flour, salt, paprika and Tabasco. Add water. Cook, stirring constantly, until thickened. *Makes about 1 cup.*

# Cocktail Sauce

⅓ cup chili sauce
½ cup catchup
1 teaspoon minced onion
1 ½ teaspoons tarragon vinegar
1 tablespoon lemon juice
¼ teaspoon salt
Dash pepper
Dash cayenne
1 small garlic clove

Combine all ingredients. Chill. Remove garlic clove before serving. *Makes about ¾ cup.*

# Basic Cream Sauce

2 tablespoons butter or margarine
2 tablespoons flour
1 cup light cream
½ teaspoon salt
⅛ teaspoon pepper

Melt butter; blend in flour. Stir in cream. Stir until mixture boils and thickens. Cook about 3 minutes longer, stirring occasionally. Add seasonings. Cover, set over hot water to keep hot. *Makes about 1 cup.*

*Variations of Cream Sauce:*

*Savory Cream Sauce*—Add 1 teaspoon each minced onion, parsley, pimiento and celery.

*Cream Horseradish Sauce*—Add ½ cup drained, prepared horseradish and a dash of Tabasco sauce.

*Cream Caper Sauce*—Add 2 to 4 tablespoons chopped capers and additional salt to taste.
58

# Cranberry And Horseradish Relish

| | |
|---|---|
| 1 pound fresh cranberries | ⅓ cup prepared horseradish |
| ½ cup sugar | 1 teaspoon lemon juice |

Put cranberries through food chopper, using medium knife. Add remaining ingredients. Chill several hours. Add more sugar if necessary. *Makes about 3 cups.*

# Cumberland Sauce

| | |
|---|---|
| 1 jar (10 ounces) red currant jelly | ¼ cup orange juice |
| ½ teaspoon dry mustard | 1 tablespoon lemon juice |
| 1 tablespoon grated orange peel | ⅛ teaspoon ground ginger |
| 1 tablespoon grated lemon peel | |

Combine ingredients in saucepan. Heat, stirring occasionally, until jelly melts. Cook until mixture is smooth. *Makes about 1 cup.*

# Currant-Orange Sauce

| | |
|---|---|
| ½ cup currant jelly | ¾ teaspoon dry mustard |
| ¼ cup orange juice | ½ teaspoon powdered ginger |
| 1 tablespoon grated orange peel | 1 tablespoon wine vinegar |

Break up jelly with fork. Stir in remaining ingredients. If a milder flavor is desired add a little water. *Makes about ¾ cup.*

# Curry Sauce I

| | | | |
|---|---|---|---|
| ¼ | cup butter or margarine | 2 | teaspoons sugar |
| ⅓ | cup finely chopped onion | 1 | teaspoon salt |
| ¼ | cup flour | ¼ | teaspoon powdered ginger |
| 1 | tablespoon curry powder (or to taste) | ⅛ | teaspoon pepper |
| | | 2 | cups milk |
| | | 2 | teaspoons lemon juice |

Melt butter. Add onion; sauté until golden, about 5 minutes. Remove from heat. Blend in flour, curry powder, sugar, salt, ginger and pepper; stir until smooth. Add milk, a little at a time, stirring after each addition. Bring to boiling point, stirring constantly. Reduce heat; simmer 1 minute. Stir in lemon juice. *Makes about 2 ¼ cups.*

# Curry Sauce II

| | | | |
|---|---|---|---|
| ½ | medium-sized onion, chopped | 2 | teaspoons curry powder |
| 1 | small garlic clove, minced | ½ | teaspoon light brown sugar |
| ½ | teaspoon powdered ginger | 1 ½ | tablespoons flour |
| 1 | tablespoon butter or margarine | ¼ | teaspoon salt |
| | | 1 | cup chicken stock |

Sauté onion, garlic, ginger and butter in saucepan until onion is slightly browned. Stir in curry powder and brown sugar; continue stirring and cooking for 1 minute. Stir in flour and salt. Add chicken stock gradually; cook, stirring, until sauce is thickened. Cook over low heat for 10 minutes, stirring often. Strain. Serve hot or cold. *Makes about 1 ⅓ cups.*

# Dill Sauce

1 cup dairy sour cream
1 tablespoon minced parsley
1 tablespoon lemon juice
1 teaspoon chopped chives, fresh or freeze-dried
1 teaspoon grated onion
Chopped dill, fresh or dried, to taste.

Combine all ingredients; mix well. *Makes about 1 cup.*

# Drawn Butter

Slowly melt ½ cup butter in saucepan. Let stand for a few minutes until clear part can be spooned off into serving dish (a baster makes this easy). Serve warm. *Makes about ½ cup.*

***Lemon Butter:***
Add 2 tablespoons strained lemon juice to butter in serving dish.

# Fluffy Mustard Sauce

3 eggs, separated
¼ cup firmly packed brown sugar
1 tablespoon dry mustard
½ cup vinegar
½ cup consommé
½ teaspoons salt
Few grains pepper

Beat egg yolks; combine with sugar and mustard in top of small double boiler. Add vinegar and consommé; heat thoroughly. Add seasonings. Beat egg whites stiff; fold in egg yolk mixture. Cook about 5 minutes longer. *Makes 6 servings.*

# Garden Dressing

4 tablespoons lemon juice
3 tablespoons tarragon vinegar
⅔ cup vegetable oil
1 ½ teaspoons salt
Few grains cayenne

1 teaspoon sugar
½ teaspoon paprika
1 tablespoon chopped parsley
1 tablespoon chopped water cress
1 tablespoon finely cut chives

Combine all ingredients; stir until salt and sugar dissolve. Let stand ½ hour. Mix well before serving. *Makes 6 servings.*

# Golden Mint Sauce

¾ cup mayonnaise
¼ cup snipped mint leaves

½ teaspoon dry mustard
1 hard-cooked egg yolk, sieved

Combine all ingredients. Let stand one hour before using. *Makes about 1 cup.*

# Hollandaise Sauce

¾ cup butter
1 ½ tablespoons lemon juice

3 egg yolks, well beaten
Dash of salt
Dash of cayenne

Divide butter into 3 pieces; put 1 piece in top of small double boiler, add lemon juice and egg yolks. Set over hot water (not boiling); cook slowly, beating constantly with wire whisk. When butter is melted, add second piece of butter and, as mixture thickens, add the third piece and cook until thickened, stirring constantly. Remove immediately from water, add salt and cayenne. Serve at once. If sauce curdles add hot water by the teaspoon, stirring vigorously. *Makes about ¾ cup.*

## Horseradish Sauce I

| | |
|---|---|
| 1 cup dairy sour cream | 2 tablespoons chopped chives, fresh or freeze-dried |
| 1 tablespoon prepared horse-radish | |

Combine all ingredients; mix well. *Makes about 1 cup.*

## Horseradish Sauce II

| | |
|---|---|
| 1 cup dairy sour cream | 1 small onion, minced |
| 6 tablespoons prepared horse-radish | ¼ teaspoon freshly ground black pepper |

Combine sour cream, horseradish, onion and pepper in a small bowl, beating until well-blended. Chill. *Makes about 2 cups.*

## Horseradish Sauce III

| | |
|---|---|
| 1 cup dairy sour cream | 2 tablespoons minced dill pickle |
| 2 tablespoons prepared horse-radish | ½ teaspoon salt |
| | ⅛ teaspoon paprika |

Combine all ingredients. Chill. *Makes about 1 cup.*

# Hot Wine Mayonnaise

1 tablespoon in-
stant minced
onion
¼ cup sauterne

1 tablespoon lemon
juice
¾ cup mayonnaise
2 tablespoons
chopped parsley

Add onion to wine; let stand 10 minutes. Add remaining ingredients. Heat over hot, not boiling,
water. *Makes about 1 cup.*

# Louis Sauce

1 cup mayon-
naise
⅓ cup chili sauce
1 small onion,
grated
1 tablespoon
chopped parsley
Dash cayenne
1 tablespoon tar-
ragon vinegar

2 tablespoons
chopped stuffed
olives
½ teaspoon Worces-
tershire sauce
½ teaspoon pre-
pared horse-
radish

Combine all ingredients. Chill. *Makes about 1⅔
cups.*

# Mint Sauce For Lamb

½ cup white
vinegar
⅓ cup sugar

Fresh mint
leaves

Heat vinegar and sugar in small saucepan, stirring until sugar is dissolved. Snip enough mint

leaves coarsely to measure ½ cup. Pour hot vinegar mixture over mint in small bowl; let stand, covered, several hours. Before serving, strain sauce; discard mint. Snip more fresh mint leaves to measure ¼ cup. Add to sauce. Serve at room temperature. *Makes about ⅔ cup.*

## Mousseline Sauce

| | |
|---|---|
| 2 tablespoons butter or margarine | ¼ cup cream |
| 2 tablespoons flour | Salt and pepper to taste |
| ¾ cup chicken stock | 1 ½ teaspoons lemon juice |
| 1 egg yolk | |

Melt butter or margarine over low heat; add flour; stir until well blended. Remove from heat. Stir in stock gradually; return to heat. Cook, stirring constantly, until thick and smooth. Beat egg yolk slightly; add cream and a little of the hot stock. Add to remaining stock; cook over very low heat for 2 minutes, stirring constantly. Season to taste. Remove from heat; add lemon juice. *Makes about 1 cup.*

## Mustard Mayonnaise

| | |
|---|---|
| 2 cups mayonnaise | ¼ cup vinegar |
| ⅓ cup prepared mustard | |

Combine mayonnaise, mustard and vinegar in a small bowl, beat until well-blended; chill. *Makes about 2½ cups.*

# Raw Apple Relish

| | |
|---|---|
| 3 tart apples | 2 stalks celery |
| 1 green pepper | 1 ½ teaspoons salt |
| 1 sweet red pepper | ¾ cup sugar |
| 1 small onion | ⅓ cup lemon juice |

Chop apples, peppers, onion and celery. Add remaining ingredients. Mix well. Cover; chill thoroughly. *Makes about 3 cups.*

# Bearnaise Sauce I

| | |
|---|---|
| ⅓ cup water | 3 egg yolks, |
| 1 ½ tablespoons tar- | slightly beaten |
| ragon vinegar | ¼ cup butter or |
| Few grains coarse | margarine |
| black pepper | ¼ teaspoon salt |
| ½ onion, sliced | ¼ teaspoon paprika |

Combine water, vinegar, pepper and onion in small saucepan. Heat to boiling point. Remove onion. Place egg yolks in top of double boiler. Add hot liquid gradually. Cook over hot, not boiling, water, stirring constantly, until mixture begins to thicken. Remove from heat. Add butter, 1 tablespoon at a time, salt and paprika. Stir vigorously. Serve immediately. *Makes about 1 cup.*

# Bearnaise Sauce II

| | |
|---|---|
| ½ cup tarragon | ½ teaspoon dried |
| vinegar | tarragon leaves |
| ¼ cup dry white wine | 3 egg yolks |
| 1 tablespoon | ½ cup butter or |
| minced onion | margarine |

Combine vinegar, wine, onion and tarragon in small saucepan. Bring just to boiling. Reduce heat;

simmer, uncovered, until liquid is reduced to about ⅓ cup, 8 to 10 minutes. Strain into top of double boiler, discarding onion and tarragon leaves. Beat in egg yolks. Cook over hot, not boiling, water, beating constantly, until mixture is as thick as mayonnaise. Beat in butter, 1 tablespoon at a time, beating well after each addition to melt butter. Serve at once. *Makes about 1 cup.*

## Creole Sauce

½ cup finely chopped onions
1 garlic clove, finely chopped
¼ cup chopped green pepper
2 tablespoons vegetable oil
1 can (1 pound 12 ounces) tomatoes, undrained

1 teaspoon celery seed
1 bay leaf
1 teaspoon salt
2 teaspoons sugar
½ teaspoon chili powder
1 tablespoon chopped parsley

Sauté onions, garlic and pepper in oil until tender, about 5 minutes. Add remaining ingredients; simmer, uncovered, 45 minutes, or until mixture is thickened, stirring occasionally. Strain. *Makes about 3 cups.*

## Quick Shrimp Sauce

1 can (10 ounces) frozen shrimp soup
¾ cup milk

1 teaspoon instant minced onion
Dash cayenne pepper

Combine all ingredients. Heat thoroughly. *Makes about 2 cups.*

# Mexicana Sauce

½ cup canned
  tomatoes
¼ cup chili sauce
2 tablespoons
  prepared horse-
  radish
¼ cup vinegar
1 tablespoon pre-
  pared mustard

½ teaspoon salt
Dash of pepper
½ teaspoon curry
  powder
2 tablespoons
  chopped parsley
½ teaspoon grated
  onion

Combine all ingredients in saucepan; cook slowly until thickened. Strain; cool. This sauce may be kept in refrigerator for a week. When ready to use, mix with mayonnaise using 1 part sauce to 2 parts mayonnaise. *Makes about 2¼ cups sauce after mayonnaise is added.*

# Never-Fail Hollandaise Sauce

3 egg yolks
2 tablespoons lemon
  juice

¼ teaspoon each salt,
  sugar, dry mus-
  tard and Tabasco
  sauce
½ cup very cold butter
  or margarine

Beat together egg yolks, lemon juice and seasonings in top of double boiler. Divide butter into 3 equal portions. Add one portion of butter to the egg mixture. Cook over hot water, stirring constantly, until butter is melted. Add second portion of butter, and when this is melted, repeat with third portion, stirring constantly as butter melts and sauce thickens. Remove from heat. Serve hot or at room temperature. Leftover sauce may be kept in refrigerator. *Makes about 1 cup.*

# Mornay Sauce

| | |
|---|---|
| 1 chicken bouillon cube | ¾ cup light cream |
| ¾ cup boiling water | ½ cup grated Parmesan cheese |
| ¼ cup butter or margarine | ½ cup shredded Swiss cheese |
| ¼ cup flour | |

Dissolve bouillon cube in boiling water. Melt butter in saucepan. Blend in flour; add cream. Cook, stirring constantly, until thick. Blend in bouillon and cheeses. Stir until smooth. Serve hot. *Makes about 3 cups.*

# Peanut Curry Sauce

| | |
|---|---|
| ½ cup apple jelly | 1 teaspoon curry powder (or to taste) |
| ½ cup peanut butter | |
| 1 cup water | |
| 1 teaspoon brown-gravy seasoning sauce | |

Combine ingredients in a saucepan and blend well. Bring to a boil. Simmer for 5 minutes; serve hot. *Makes about 1 cup.*

# Remoulade Sauce

| | |
|---|---|
| 1 cup mayonnaise | 1 teaspoon dried tarragon |
| 1 hard-cooked egg, chopped fine | 1 teaspoon anchovy paste |
| 1 teaspoon dry mustard | 1 teaspoon capers |
| 1 garlic clove, minced | |

Combine all ingredients; mix well. *Makes about 1¼ cups.*

69

# Piquante Sauce

1 cup dairy sour cream
1 package dry onion soup mix
3 egg yolks
1 teaspoon lemon juice
½ teaspoon Worcestershire sauce
Salt and pepper, to taste

Blend sour cream and soup mix; stir in egg yolks, lemon juice, Worcestershire sauce and seasonings. Cook over low heat, stirring constantly, until sauce starts to thicken slightly. *Do not boil.* Remove from heat; continue to stir as sauce thickens. Cool before serving. *Makes about 1½ cups.*

# Vert Sauce

1 slice white bread
¼ cup vinegar
½ teaspoon anchovy paste
1 cup minced parsley
1½ teaspoons chopped capers
2 garlic cloves, crushed
1½ teaspoons grated onion
4 teaspoons vegetable oil
½ teaspoon sugar
2 tablespoons vinegar

Trim crusts from bread; soak bread in ¼ cup vinegar. Stir in anchovy paste, parsley, capers, garlic onion, oil and sugar; mix well. Beat into a smooth paste. Stir in 2 tablespoons vinegar. *Makes about 1¼ cups.*

***Variations:***
Add 2 tablespoons coarsely chopped pitted green olives, or chopped sweet gherkins or chopped green pepper.

70

# Savory Green Sauce

½ cup mayonnaise
2 tablespoons finely chopped parsley
¼ cup finely chopped chives

¼ cup finely chopped water cress
2 teaspoons grated onion
2 teaspoons tarragon vinegar

Combine all ingredients; blend well. *Makes about 1 cup.*

# Seafood Sauce

¾ cup chili sauce or catchup
2 tablespoons prepared horseradish, drained
1 tablespoon lemon juice

⅛ teaspoon pepper
½ teaspoon salt
½ teaspoon Worcestershire sauce
Dash Tabasco sauce

Combine all ingredients. Refrigerate until well chilled. *Makes about 1 cup.*

# Sour Cream Sauce

1 cup dairy sour cream
2 tablespoons vinegar
1 tablespoon sugar

1 teaspoon salt
¼ teaspoon paprika
1 teaspoon dry mustard

Whip cream until it reaches the consistency of soft custard. Combine vinegar, sugar and seasonings; add gradually to cream, beating lightly. *Makes about 1½ cups sauce.*

71

# Sea Goddess Sauce

1 garlic clove
3 tablespoons
   minced anchovies
¼ cup cut chives
1 tablespoon lemon
   juice
1 tablespoon tarra-
   gon wine vinegar

½ cup dairy sour
   cream
1 cup mayonnaise
⅓ cup finely chopped
   parsley
Salt and coarse
   black pepper to taste

Grate or mince garlic very fine. Combine with remaining ingredients in the order given. Chill thoroughly. *Makes about 2 cups.*


# Soubise Sauce

2 cups sliced
   onions
3 tablespoons but-
   ter or margarine
3 tablespoons flour

1 cup milk or 1 cup
   chicken or veal
   stock
½ cup cream
Salt and pepper
   to taste

Let onions stand in boiling water 5 minutes;
drain. Melt butter or margarine over low heat; add
onions. Cover, simmer about 10 minutes or until
soft but not browned. Add flour; stir until well
blended. Remove from heat. Stir in milk or stock
gradually; return to heat. Cook, stirring constantly,
until thick and smooth. Cook over hot water 20 to
30 minutes. Force through coarse sieve; add cream;
reheat. Season to taste. *Makes about 1½ cups.*

# Steak Sauce

¼ cup vinegar
2 tablespoons sugar
1 tablespoon prepared mustard
¼ teaspoon coarsely ground black pepper
1 ½ teaspoons salt
⅛ teaspoon Tabasco sauce
1 lemon, thickly sliced
1 medium onion, sliced
¼ cup butter or margarine
2 tablespoons Worcestershire sauce
½ cup Burgundy

Combine all but last 3 ingredients; simmer 20 minutes. Add butter, Worcestershire and wine; bring to boil. Strain. *Makes about 1½ cups.*

# Sweet-Sour Sauce

½ cup pineapple juice
2 tablespoons vinegar
2 tablespoons brown sugar
Few grains pepper
½ teaspoon paprika
1 chicken bouillon cube
1 teaspoon prepared mustard
1 tablespoon cornstarch
¼ cup water

Combine all ingredients except cornstarch and water in small saucepan. Cook until bouillon cube is dissolved. Combine cornstarch and water. Stir into hot liquid. Cook, stirring constantly, until clear and thick. *Makes about 1 cup.*

# Tartar Sauce I

1 tablespoon
chopped stuffed
olives
1 tablespoon
minced parsley

1 tablespoon
chopped capers
1 tablespoon
chopped sweet
gherkins
1 cup mayonnaise

Fold olives, parsley, capers and gherkins into mayonnaise. *Makes about 1¼ cups.*

# Tartar Sauce II

1 teaspoon minced
onion
2 teaspoons chopped
sweet pickle
1 teaspoon chopped
green olives

1 tablespoon
capers
1 tablespoon minced
parsley
¾ cup mayonnaise
1 tablespoon tarragon vinegar

Combine first 4 ingredients; drain thoroughly; add parsley; fold into mayonnaise. Stir in vinegar. *Makes about ¾ cup.*

# Tartar Sauce III

1 cup mayonnaise
¼ cup minced dill
pickle
2 tablespoons
minced parsley
1 teaspoon lemon
juice

½ teaspoon grated
onion
¼ teaspoon Worcestershire sauce
1 tablespoon capers

Combine all ingredients. Chill. *Makes about 1⅓ cups.*

74

# Tarragon Caper Sauce

2 egg yolks
½ teaspoon dried
  tarragon leaves
1 cup dairy sour
  cream
1 bay leaf,
  crumbled
¼ teaspoon minced
  garlic
½ teaspoon salt
1 tablespoon capers,
  drained

Beat egg yolks until thick and lemon-colored. Stir in tarragon. Heat sour cream, bay leaf and garlic slowly, until bubbles form around edge. Strain; discard garlic and bay leaf. Pour sour cream back into saucepan. Pour a little hot sour cream into egg yolks, stirring; add to remaining sour cream. Bring just to boiling point, over low heat, stirring constantly. Add salt and capers. *Makes about 1¼ cups.*

# Vinegar Sauce

2 tablespoons but-
  ter or margarine
2 tablespoons flour
¼ cup dry mustard
½ cup sugar
¾ teaspoon salt
¾ cup boiling water
¾ cup vinegar
¾ cup mayonnaise
4 small sweet
  pickles, chopped

Melt butter over low heat; add flour, mustard, sugar and salt; stir until well blended. Remove from heat. Stir in boiling water and vinegar slowly; return to heat; cook, stirring constantly, until thick and smooth. Stir in mayonnaise and pickles gradually. Blend well; heat. This sauce will keep in a refrigerator and may be reheated. *Makes about 2⅓ cups.*

# Whole Cranberry Sauce

2 cups sugar
2 cups water

4 cups fresh
cranberries

Combine sugar and water in saucepan; stir over medium heat until sugar dissolves. Boil 5 minutes. Add cranberries. Boil without stirring until all skin pop (about 5 minutes). Cool. *Makes about 4½ cups.*

# 6.
# Dessert Fondues

ODDLY enough the first dessert fondue, made with Swiss chocolate, originated in this country. It soon found its way to Switzerland where it is now enormously popular.

The classic version is still made with Swiss Toblerone chocolate, but an excellent version can be prepared with semi-sweet chocolate pieces, while interesting and delicious fondues can be made with chocolate crunch bars and hazelnut milk chocolate bars.

Fruit is delicious for dunking into the smooth chocolate sauce. Try slices of apple, pineapple chunks, seedless grapes, mandarin orange sections or tangerine sections, strawberries, banana chunks, sections of seedless oranges, etc. Be sure the fruit is well drained.

77

Or you might prefer lady fingers, chunks of angel food or sponge cake, cubes of pound cake or tiny cream puffs.

Spear the food on long-handled fondue forks and swirl it in the warm chocolate sauce. Delectable!

Recipes for baked dessert fondues are given also.

Invite two or three friends to "come for coffee and dessert" and serve chocolate fondue. Or, serve it after an evening of music or TV viewing. Don't try to serve it after having served another fondue for the main course, but enjoy it for itself alone.

## Classic Chocolate Fondue

| | |
|---|---|
| 3 bars (3 ounces each) Toblerone chocolate | ½ cup whipping cream |
| | 2 tablespoons kirsch* |

Break up the chocolate into triangular pieces. Combine all ingredients in small chafing dish, chocolate fondue pot or top of small double-boiler. Stir over direct low heat until chocolate is melted and mixture is smooth. Set over hot water to keep warm while serving.

*Or brandy, cognac, light dry rum, applejack or 1 tablespoon instant coffee or ¼ teaspoon each cinnamon and allspice.

## Chocolate Fondue American-Style

| | |
|---|---|
| 1 package (6 ounces) semi-sweet chocolate morsels | 2 tablespoons whipping cream |
| 1 tablespoon water | 2 tablespoons brandy |
| | Dash cinnamon (optional) |

Combine morsels and water in preheated chocolate fondue pot, top of small double-boiler or small chafing dish. Stir over heat, until chocolate melts and mixture is smooth. Add remaining ingredients; stir until well blended. Keep warm. Serve the same as Classic Chocolate Fondue.

## Baked Chocolate Fondue

| | |
|---|---|
| 2 squares unsweetened chocolate | 1 tablespoon butter or margarine |
| 1 cup milk | ½ cup sugar |
| 1 cup soft bread crumbs | ¼ teaspoon salt |
| | 3 eggs, separated |

Break chocolate into small pieces; add to milk; heat until melted; stir until blended. Add crumbs, butter, sugar and salt. Beat egg yolks slightly; stir in a little of the hot milk mixture; add to remaining milk mixture. Cool. Beat egg whites until stiff; fold into cooled mixture. Turn into greased baking dish; bake at 350° about 40 minutes. Serve with whipped cream. *Makes 6 servings.*

## Baked Date Fondue

| | |
|---|---|
| 1 cup milk | ⅓ cup sugar |
| 1 cup soft bread crumbs | ¼ teaspoon salt |
| | 3 eggs, separated |
| 1 tablespoon butter or margarine | ¾ cup chopped dates |

Scald milk; add crumbs, butter, sugar and salt. Beat egg yolks slightly; stir in a little of the hot milk mixture; return to remaining hot milk mixture. Cool to lukewarm. Beat egg whites until stiff; fold in chopped dates and cooled egg mixture. Pour into greased baking dish; bake at 350° for about 40 minutes. *Makes 6 servings.*

# Baked Fruit Fondue

Follow recipe for Baked Date Fondue above, omitting dates. Fold 1 cup chopped cooked, canned or fresh fruit or berries into cooled egg mixture before folding into egg whites. If desired, substitute fruit juice for part of milk. Peaches, apricots, blueberries or raspberries are all good choices.

# Peach Macaroon Fondue

| | |
|---|---|
| ⅓ cup butter or margarine | 1 cup finely chopped fresh peaches |
| ½ cup sugar | ¼ teaspoon salt |
| 3 eggs, separated | ¼ teaspoon almond flavoring |
| 1 cup dry macaroon crumbs | |

Cream butter until soft; add sugar gradually. Beat until light and fluffy. Add egg yolks, one at a time, beating well after each addition. Add macaroon crumbs and chopped peaches. Beat egg whites until foamy; sprinkle with salt; beat until stiff but not dry. Fold into egg yolk mixture; add almond flavoring. Pour into well-greased 1½-quart casserole. Bake at 325° for 30 to 40 minutes or until browned. Serve immediately from the baking dish. *Makes 6 servings.*

# INDEX